From the desktops of Andy and Gil Leaf

One of the most important lessons our father taught us is the value of reading. The exhilaration of turning a page and having words leap out, begging to be uttered and embraced, is a profound experience that is permanently etched in the mind. This was his message to every child. A springboard for the imagination, a book can be educational *and* fun.

It is a huge joy that the key to the amusing, creative, and engaging world of our father can once again be found on bookshelves. He would be tremendously pleased and satisfied to know that today, nearly seventy years and one century later, his words still have resonance—words that will be fondly remembered by generations past, and words that will be savored, chuckled over, and read countless times by a new generation of curious, inquisitive, and impressionable young eyes.

Your Name Here

READING CAN BE FUN

First published in the United States of America in 2004
by UNIVERSE PUBLISHING
A Division of Rizzoli International Publications, Inc.
300 Park Avenue South
New York, NY 10010
www.rizzoliusa.com

2004 2005 2006 2007 2008 / 10 9 8 7 6 5 4 3 2 1

Printed in China

ISBN: 0-7893-1203-4

Library of Congress Catalog Control Number: 2004103281

Cover design: Headcase Design
www.headcasedesign.com

READING CAN BE FUN

Munro Leaf

UNIVERSE

READING CAN BE FUN—

Not so very long ago, you
knew how to say only one
word, and that one word was

WHAAA!

It was a good, useful word for you
because it could mean:
I'm hungry   or   *I'm thirsty*
I'm too hot   or   *too cold*
or *There's a pin sticking me!*
or maybe
I'm tired of sitting here all by myself.
I want somebody to come and play
with me right now!

Whatever you meant,
you said

WHAAA!

and somebody else had to guess just
which one you did mean.

As you grew older, you found out that people made different kinds of noises with their mouths when they meant different things.

The noise YES meant something different from the noise NO all right, and you soon found it out.

After a while you began to know what a lot of those word noises meant that other people made. And when you began to make them yourself, you had begun to talk.

Almost everybody learns to talk before he learns to write or read. In fact, people could talk to each other way back in the days of the cave men.

They still didn't know how to read or write though for thousands and thousands of years.

The first writing we have found that was done by people long, long ago was picture writing that looked something like this—

Now if you had read this kind of picture writing you were supposed to know that a man named Zuzu left home. He hunted for six days until he found a bear over near the mountains and he killed it.

Well, you can easily see that anybody

could get all mixed up reading picture writing. We might think those six suns up there for six days might be six moons and mean that he took six months to find that bear. What's more, if the writer couldn't draw very well, you might think it was a hairy pig he found and not a bear at all. And worse yet, maybe the person standing on the dead bear was Zuzu's brother instead of Zuzu.

Anyway you can see how you might get all mixed up with picture writing, can't you?

Well, after a while, thank goodness, some people thought up a much simpler and better way to write. And the way that they did it is the way we still do it now.

Instead of drawing pictures of what happened, they drew little pictures of the sounds or noises somebody would make if he were *telling* you what happened.

They decided that they could draw little pictures that stood for the different sounds people made when they talked. Then we could look at those pictures and we would know just what they had said.

We call those little pictures of different sounds

LETTERS

like A and B and C and D or T and Y and I and G and O and L.

When we put some of them together in little bunches, we call those bunches

WORDS

like the word CAT or DOG or BOY or GIRL.

Now you might easily think that it would take an awful lot of letter pictures to write all the different words that people say **BUT** one of the nicest surprises about learning to read is that there are only 26 different letter pictures in all the books you will ever read. Sometimes we print them as BIG letters and sometimes as little letters, but they mean the same sounds, big or little, and here they are—

A or a	B or b	C or c	D or d
E e	F f	G g	H h
I i	J j	K k	L l
M m	N n	O o	P p
Q q	R r	S s	T t
U u	V v	W w	X x
	Y y	Z z	

Anyone who ever went to school knows that we use only 26 different letters to write all our words. **BUT** here is something most people don't know. We make only 44 different kinds of noises or sounds when we say all the words we ever use. **SO** when you learn which ones of the 44

A B C D
AND THE OTHER
LETTERS ARE CALLED
THE ALPHABET

sounds to make whenever you see words

made out of bunches of these 26 letter

pictures, then

YOU CAN READ.

But learning to read isn't something you can do in one day. You have to think and you have to do some work to learn to read. So some lazy people ask "Oh, why should I learn to read?—it's too much bother."

They say, "If I can talk to people and see movies and listen to the radio and watch television without knowing how to read, why should I read—what good will it do me anyway?"

Now, people who say, "Why should I read?" may sound silly to you, but let's see just what the answers are to that question—

WHY SHOULD I READ?

Most of us
want to grow.

We don't want our BODIES to stay
baby sized when we get older. You would
feel kind of foolish, if when you were
twelve years old you were
still only about two feet
high and pushing around
the floor on a baby
scooter. Wouldn't you?
So, what do we do?

WE EAT

and drink—milk—mush—vegetables—hot dogs—hamburgers—cereals—roast beef—ham and eggs—ice cream—cake and many other things.

Our bodies—our bones—our teeth grow—our muscles get stronger and we get bigger all over. We know that we have to eat the right things if our bodies are going to grow the way we want them to.

Well, our minds have to grow too, if we are going to have any fun in life.

We have to learn to think and understand more and more, and do things for ourselves instead of having everything done for us. If our minds didn't grow too, we would go around when we were twelve years old still squawking WHAAA for everything. We wouldn't even know enough to feed or dress ourselves.

And just as we have to eat good food

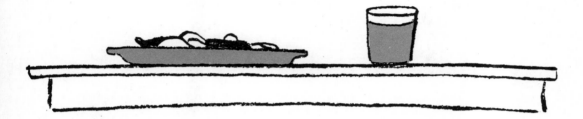

to have our bodies grow well—
so we have to get

GOOD IDEAS

to have our minds grow well.

Did you ever think about this?

While we are growing up, where do
we get the food we need for our growing
bodies? And where do we get the ideas
we need for our growing minds?

The answer is the same for both questions.
We get both, food and ideas, from other
people.

And this is what is IMPORTANT—
the kind of person that you are going to
be depends on what kind of food and
what kind of ideas you get from those
other people.

At first, when we are little, we get almost all of our food and our ideas from our mothers and fathers.

Most of us are lucky, because we have mothers and fathers who love us and they try hard to see that we get good food and good ideas.

By watching them and copying the way they do things and listening to what they tell us, we learn to

walk

dress ourselves

brush our teeth

feed ourselves

wash ourselves

talk to
people

comb our hair

help others

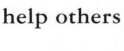

be kind to animals

We get all kinds of good ideas from them that help our minds to grow. After a while we start to meet and know other people. Brothers, sisters and play-mates all begin to give us more ideas.

Sometimes some of the ideas we get from them aren't such good ones—but they make us think, and after a while we can tell the good from the bad ones.

We have older friends too—Grand-mothers and Grand-fathers, Aunts and Uncles, neighbors

and friends of our mothers and fathers. From them we learn more and more about

how people think and what they do to get along to-gether and have a good time.

When we go to school we meet new friends and teachers. Hardly a day goes by in which we don't get new ideas.

By this time most of us have met a lot of people—people who talk to us and tell us things that we want to know.

BUT WHEN WE LEARN TO READ

all of a sudden we know what thousands of new friends all around us are saying to us. They are new friends that we have never seen.

It's almost like magic when we know what those letter pictures and words mean and we can read.

We see a sign at a dangerous street corner and it says—

One of our wise friends we have never seen has told us something we needed to know.

And because we know how to read what he said, he no longer has to be there to tell us with his mouth.

Knowing how to read is almost like having a private telephone all your own. People who write can tell you things that you want to know though they are thousands of miles away from you. Or maybe they have not even been

alive for hundreds and hundreds of years.
They can still tell you things through the
books they wrote.

When you know how to read you can
have for your own friends the wisest and
the best and greatest people who have
ever lived in the world.

YOU

So you can see how reading will help you to get ready to be a grown up.

You can find out what is happening all over the world, the way your parents do when they read the newspaper or a magazine.

Reading will help you with your work the way it helps your parents to take care of your family and your home. Because they can read they know where to buy things. They can tell what they cost just by

looking at the signs on them and they don't have to ask some-body to tell them.

If they want to cook something extra nice for you they can read how to do it in a cookbook. If they do just what it says to in the book, it is like having one of the best cooks in the world to tell them how.

You can read how to make things like model jet planes or cars by following written directions. You work the same way engineers do when they build bridges or doctors do when they save people's lives. You read to learn.

You can read about hundreds of ways to make things and do things that are fun. Reading will help you to get ready to be happy grown ups who do what they like best.

The reading that you do in school and college and in working will be useful to you. It will help to make you the kind of person you want to be when you're grown up

BUT

there is still another reason for reading and that is

READING JUST FOR FUN

When people first read stories to you,

you learn what fun it is to meet the new

friends in books. You meet animal

friends as well as men and women and

boys and girls. What they do and how they feel seems almost as real as what happens to you or the boy next door.

Making believe that you are doing things anywhere at any time with friends in stories is one of the best ways in the world to have fun.

All you need is a good book and a comfortable place to sit quietly, and you

find out what happened to Peter
Rabbit in Mr. McGregor's garden, or
how Jim Hawkins sailed with pirates.
When we haven't quite learned how to
read for ourselves yet,
we can share our story-
book friends with the
people who read for us.

All our lives one of the nicest things about having friends is having others know them too. There are so many friends waiting in books to meet you that story time can hardly ever seem half long enough.

As we grow older and can read more and more to ourselves, we find in books new companions of all kinds and times and places. It's almost like having your  own private rocket space ship. A good book can carry you to a meeting spot anywhere in a flash and you can join in on adventures with

people and animals who are doing
things that will fill your hours with
real pleasure.

Life in strange and faraway places becomes as real as a trip to the corner drugstore. The people we meet in the stories we read often become so close and alive to us that we wish that they lived next door.

No ocean is too wide, no jungle too thick, no northland too frozen, no ancient castle wall too strong to keep us from riding our own book trails to excitement, adventure and fun.

Books not only can take us to lands of make believe where anything can happen, but they also make friends for us of the great people who have really lived and helped to make our world the kind of place it is.

The whole wonderful story of the past and the interesting days we live in now take on new color and meaning when we learn more about them through the books we read. And if you like to imagine what the future holds with new adventures of science into space and the great days ahead, there are books to lead you in your most exciting guessing.

These friends in books are friends for life. You will find that you share them with others wherever you go and whatever you do.

And the wonderful part of it all is that without getting out of your chair, you can go everywhere with them, do most anything you want to with them, and still be home in time for

READING CAN BE FUN

THESE NEXT PAGES

ARE ABOUT

BOOKS THAT

I HAVE READ

AND

THE

PICTURES

ARE

DRAWN

BY